MEN-AT-ARMS SERIES

EDITOR: MARTIN WINDROW
ALBAN BOOK SERVICES

The Austro-Hungarian Army of the Napoleonic Wars

Richard de Unger
The Manor House
Ham, Richmond, Surrey

Text by ALBERT SEATON

Colour plates by R. OTTENFELD

OSPREY PUBLISHING LIMITED

Published in 1973 by
Osprey Publishing Ltd, P.O. Box 25,
707 Oxford Road, Reading, Berkshire
© Copyright 1973 Osprey Publishing Ltd

In the preparation of the plates, illustrations and
text acknowledgment is made to *Die Österreichische
Armee* by O. Teuber (Vienna 1895–1904). All the
photographs are reproduced by courtesy of the
Keeper, the Library of the Victoria and Albert
Museum (Photographer Berkhamsted Photographic,
Berkhamsted, Hertfordshire).

ISBN 0 85045 147 7

Printed in Great Britain by
Jarrold & Sons Ltd, Norwich

Introduction

The Austro-Hungarian Empire dated from only 1804. Before then, the Emperor Francis I had been Emperor Francis II of the Holy Roman Empire, not of Austria-Hungary. Whereas France and Britain were homogeneous states and Spain had a form of traditional unity, the Austro-Hungarian Empire had none. For it embraced Germans, Hungarians, Czechs, Slovaks, Croats, Ukrainians, Poles, Russians, Rumanians, Italians, and Belgians with no bond except that of a common emperor.

Officer in a Roquelor coat, 1790

Happy Austria makes Marriages

Austria originated as a tiny German eastern frontier duchy in Charlemagne's *Ostmark*, and Vienna, its capital, had no significance until the tenth century. Its earlier rulers, the Habsburgs, were fortunate in that they enlarged their domains usually by clever marriages. In 1273 Rudolf of

Habsburg, because of his lack of authority and pretension, was elected as King of Germany and Holy Roman Emperor, and from 1440 onwards it became customary to elect an Austrian Habsburg to the throne. The regal and imperial titles, usually held at the same time, were, however, largely without substance, for although the Empire was said to be derived from the Roman Empire of Charlemagne or, more correctly speaking, from the German Empire of Otto the Great, succession depended on the votes of the German electoral princes; the rulers of the many hundreds of German states within the Empire were in fact independent. The imperial title had merely a traditional and prestige value.

Yet, by the end of the fifteenth century, Austria was already the most powerful single state within

3

the borders of the old Empire, for Upper and Lower Austria had joined with Styria, Carinthia, and the Tyrol. Advantageous foreign marriages brought Austria, Burgundy, and the Netherlands and finally, under the Emperor Charles V, Spain, Milan, Sardinia, and the Two Sicilies (South Italy and Sicily). When Charles abdicated in 1556 he split the Habsburg's Spanish and German possessions, allotting the first to his son and the second to his brother. But even this did not limit the power or fortune of the Austrian Habsburgs since the brother Ferdinand, already Archduke of Austria, succeeded to the imperial title and became a successful claimant by marriage to the two elective kingdoms of Bohemia and Hungary. By 1648, the date of the Treaty of Westphalia, Austria held as

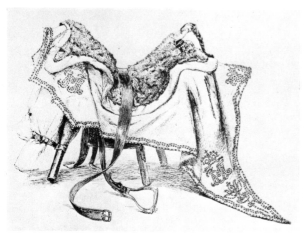

Hussar saddlery showing pelt, shabrack, and pistol holsters, 1790

part of its hereditary lands about a third of the territory within the German Empire, and included Bohemia, Moravia, and Silesia.

The greater part of Hungary had been occupied by the Ottoman Sultan for a century and a half, until 1699, but when the Turks were finally forced back south of the Danube and the Sava, Transylvania was arbitrarily detached from Hungary and ruled directly from Vienna. Hungary remained as an independent kingdom, but the only kings elected were in fact Habsburgs.

Hungary itself had a multi-racial population. The main element was Hungarian or Magyar, a race with no affinity to German or Slav, but the very large foreign indigenous or immigrant minorities, Rumanian, German, Pole, Ukrainian, and Croat, were in some areas soon to become majority nationalities. Long Turkish occupation, poor education and the existence of a feudal-type aristocracy, exempt from taxation and military service, had left the country primitive and divided.

After the War of the Spanish Succession, in which Austria played a major part, the Habsburgs were ceded by the Treaty of Utrecht in 1715 the Spanish Netherlands, Naples, Sardinia, and Milan. Austria ranked with France and Britain as one of the most powerful states in Europe.

In the seventeenth century the Austrian hegemony within the German confederation had suffered a set-back by the conversion of much of north Germany to the Protestant religion and by the Thirty Years War. Yet the only principalities in a position even to challenge Austrian leadership were Bavaria, Saxony, and Brandenburg; of these Brandenburg was generally considered to be the weakest. During the course of the century, however, Brandenburg attracted to its *Mark* and to its newly won territories in East Prussia immigrant populations from Holland and the Rhineland. Even so, its total population did not exceed four million. But energetic and capable Prussian rulers reorganized the government, finance, agriculture, education, and the army. In 1701 the Elector of Brandenburg, with the prior agreement of the Austrian Emperor, had himself styled King of Prussia, and by 1740 felt strong enough to challenge the Austrian primacy in Germany. The nature of the challenge was made clear by the invasion of the Austrian province of Silesia by Prussian troops.

The Austrian Emperor, Charles VI, being without a son, had succeeded in persuading the principal German rulers and the major European powers to agree to the Pragmatic Sanction, the succession of his daughter, Maria Theresa, to the Habsburg hereditary lands. The Elector of Bavaria was the only objector. But as soon as Charles died, Frederick the Great, the newly crowned King of Prussia, disregarding any earlier understanding made by his father, demanded Silesia as the price of his agreement to Maria Theresa's succession. The demand came at the same time as his troops crossed the Silesian border.

The Silesian Wars

When Frederick the Great occupied Silesia, with the support of France, Bavaria, Saxony and some of the northern princes, he hoped to present Austria and Europe with a *fait accompli*. He had misjudged, however, the temper and capabilities of the new Austrian ruler, a young married woman of twenty-three years of age. For Maria Theresa was by far the most outstanding monarch the House of Habsburg ever produced, determined, brave, far-sighted and astute, just and compassionate, absolute yet enlightened. The Elector of Bavaria had himself crowned as Holy Roman Emperor, Silesia was lost and a Franco-Bavarian force, welcomed by many of the Czech nobility, invaded Bohemia. The Austrian position appeared serious. Immediately Maria Theresa appealed as Queen of Hungary to the Hungarian Diet for aid, and this was readily forthcoming, Hungary finding over 60,000 troops for the Austro-Hungarian Army. For otherwise Austria was without allies except for Britain, and British effort was absorbed in a maritime and colonial war, its effort in Europe being limited to the payment of an annual subsidy to Vienna and the waging of intermittent land operations between Hanover and the Netherlands.

In 1742 Maria Theresa came to terms with Frederick the Great in order to drive a wedge between her enemies, and she agreed to the cession of Silesia. Prussia then went out of the war, taking Saxony with her. This left Austria free to deal with the French and the Bavarians. Bohemia was soon cleared and the new Emperor Charles Albert was driven out of his own Munich capital; an Anglo-Hanoverian force together with the Austrians won Dettingen, and France was forced back on the defensive. Austrian troops then prepared to conquer Alsace. Since Frederick distrusted the readiness with which Maria Theresa had ceded occupied Silesia, he had no wish to see France conquered or forced out of the war, for this would, he believed, leave him without allies to face Austria alone. So, waiting until the Austrian forces were committed in Alsace, he invaded Bohemia and took Prague. This was the start of the Second Silesian War. Austrian troops were withdrawn from Alsace to invade Bavaria. Frederick entered Saxony and vainly attempted a march on Vienna, winning battle after battle, holding doggedly on to Silesia but being unable to overcome the superior strength of the Austrians. The war spread to the Netherlands and Italy and lasted until 1748 when Maria Theresa was forced to reaffirm the cession of Silesia to Prussia.

Kanonier and officer of artillery, 1790–8. The *kanonier*'s leather case and pig-tails are still worn

5

A field officer and company officer of grenadiers

The Peace of Aix-la-Chapelle was not binding as far as Maria Theresa was concerned and she remained as determined as ever to regain Silesia. She had been impressed with Prussian governmental and military organization and efficiency, and she and her minister, von Haugwitz, reorganized both the Austrian civil and military administration to bring it nearer the Prussian model. Exemptions from taxation were abolished and the power to tax was vested in a single centralized body, responsible for all the German provinces, Bohemia, and Moravia; graduated income tax was taken into use. These reforms trebled the return to the exchequer, permitting the raising of a peace-time standing army of 108,000 men. Since, however, this reformed tax system was not applicable to Milan, the Netherlands, or Hungary, it resulted in Maria Theresa's German and Czecho-Slovak subjects bearing three-quarters of the cost of the military expenditure.

Both the Bohemian and the Hungarian crowns were elective. But since Maria Theresa had been much displeased at the display by the Czech nobility of anti-Austrian sentiment at the time of the foreign occupation, she had the Czech regalia removed from Prague to Vienna, in order to emphasize the permanency of the Austro-Bohemian union. Bohemian administration was centred on Vienna and the Austrian code of law was intro-

duced into the Czech courts. German became the language of the administration and was compulsorily taught in Bohemian schools. These measures were in fact a violation of the autonomous rights earlier guaranteed to Bohemia. The situation in Hungary was very different, for large numbers of Magyar troops had fought with great bravery during the Silesian Wars, and so Hungary was permitted to retain its own feudal social system (wherein the nobility continued to be exempt from taxation, tolls, and military service) and its own rather primitive administration.

It was in the field of diplomacy that Maria Theresa made her main effort to prepare Austria for a new war and she cleverly contrived to isolate Prussia from the rest of Europe while allying Austria to France and Russia. The British alliance she regarded as of little value and was evasive to London proposals that Austria should provide some defence for the British monarch's Hanoverian territories against Prussian ambitions. So London turned to an agreement with Berlin and the diplomatic somersault was complete.

Frederick the Great, uneasy at his isolation, in 1756, without warning and without consulting the British, invaded Austria's new ally, Saxony, since he was determined to strike a pre-emptive blow against the coalition which faced him. So Prussia started a new European War, the Third Silesian War, also known as the Seven Years War. Russia, France, and Sweden entered at Austria's side and during the course of the long and bitter fighting, Prussian Pomerania, East Prussia, and Brandenburg were invaded by Swedish, Russian, and Austrian forces. Berlin itself was twice occupied for a short time firstly by Austrian and then by Russo-Austrian troops. Yet Prussia, with a population of only five million, managed to remain undefeated. Frederick was of course a gifted strategist and tactician and gained a number of important victories. But he also lost a number of battles to both the Austrians and the Russians. He owed almost as much to the disunity of his enemies as to his own brilliant qualities. The French at this period had suffered a military decline and achieved little of importance except for the temporary occupation of Hanover. The Austro-Hungarian troops were staunch but their military leaders often lacked inspiration and efficiency; the Russians were obstinate but their command was erratic. It was the death of the Empress Elisabeth and the sudden withdrawal of the Russian armies which led to the rapid break-up of the enemy coalition. By 1762 Maria Theresa was isolated once more. The signing of the Treaty of Hubertusburg the next year finally lost Austria the province of Silesia. And so 'a million men had perished but not a hamlet had changed its ruler'.

THE EMPEROR JOSEPH'S FOREIGN AMBITIONS

Maria Theresa's son, Joseph, became the joint monarch of the Habsburg possessions, ruling together with his mother until her death in 1780. At home he was a radical, almost revolutionary reformer; abroad he was an old-fashioned imperialist with an insatiable appetite for territorial expansion.

Joseph feared Catherine the Great and distrusted Frederick, and he was determined either on the return to Austria of Silesia or on territorial

An officer of the transport corps wearing the earlier style of head-dress, c. 1798

compensations, and he tried, as best he was able, to set Russia and Prussia the one against the other. In 1769 and 1770 he met Frederick the Great in Silesia, in spite of his mother's condemnation of 'the immoral game', in order to secure some spoils for Austria in the partition of Poland. As a result, in 1772 by the first partition, Austria gained Galicia. But Joseph also coveted German territory. In 1777, when the Bavarian Elector died childless, he unsuccessfully tried to secure for Austria a third of Bavaria and the next year his troops crossed the frontier to enforce the claim. Prussia in return immediately invaded Bohemia and the Peace of Teschen of 1779 was brought about only on the insistence of Russia and France. Frederick the Great was so suspicious of Joseph's designs that in 1785 he formed the League of German Princes against him.

In the south-east Joseph looked for territorial aggrandizement at the expense of Turkey and in 1787 went to the Crimea to meet Catherine the Great to discuss an alliance directed against the Sultan, having as its aims the partition of the Ottoman Empire. Before his death in 1790, however, Joseph lived to reap the harvest of his own internal reforms. For, single-minded, honest, and uncompromising though he was, he lacked his mother's tact and higher moral virtues and, in spite of his good intentions, managed to alienate nearly all sections of the community within his hereditary lands. A popular revolt broke out in Belgium. He was unpopular in Hungary where he refused to have himself crowned and had had the Hungarian regalia brought to Vienna and consigned to a museum which he said was 'its proper place'; in consequence, the Hungarians called him 'the king with a hat'; he made German the official language instead of Latin. And when he tried to impose on Transylvania the Austrian census and tax system this led to peasant disorders. In 1788 the Turks attacked the Austrians as the allies of St Petersburg and defeated them.

With Joseph's death, the new Emperor, Leopold, inherited a war with Turkey and revolution and discontent in Belgium and Hungary. Leopold was a gifted and capable man and he soon brought peace to his dominions, although this lost him a measure of Hungarian support. For he relied overmuch on the secret police and the paid agitator and, since he was determined to keep in check Hungarian national aspirations, he used to Austria's advantage minority groups, Serbs, Rumanians, and the German Saxons, against the Magyars. He died after only two years of rule and was succeeded by his son, Francis, who was to rule for the next forty years, a man of different stamp from Leopold or Joseph, a primitive patriarch and reactionary bureaucrat whose activities in the early part of his reign were much taken up with unearthing and suppressing real and imaginary radical conspiracies.

Uhlan horse-holders, _c._ 1798

The Revolutionary Wars

Although the French kingdom was, at least in outward appearance, flourishing, it believed itself to be threatened with bankruptcy. In Europe the fashion, set by Maria Theresa and Frederick the Great of Prussia, was one of enlightened absolutism, it being believed, with some reason, that progress came from above and reaction from below. Louis XVI of France, who had come to the throne in 1774, was, however, entirely unfitted for monarchy, for, merely seeking popularity, he was incapable of directing events. In 1789, following the storming of the Bastille, what remained of the old forces of government were overthrown and the king and queen (a daughter of Maria Theresa) were held by the Paris mob.

There were already grounds for war between revolutionary France and the Austrian Habsburgs. Even in royalist France the Austrian Queen had not been popular. Marie Antoinette, now under restraint, sent messages to her brother pleading that he summon a European congress to deal with the French Revolution by armed force, and in August 1791 Leopold, together with the King of Prussia, issued at Pilnitz a joint declaration warning France of the consequences of any maltreatment of its monarch. Leopold had reason, too, to complain of French encouragement to the rebels in Belgium. Yet Leopold was cold and crafty, quick to meddle and threaten but slow to take any irrevocable step. For he knew that Catherine the Great wished to embroil both Austria and Prussia in the affairs of France so that she might have more elbow-room to deal with Poland. If he had interfered he might have done so effectively; but, on his sudden death, the challenge was immediately taken up by Francis, and in April 1792 the French Girondins, drunk with power and intent on identifying revolution with patriotism, tried to isolate Austria by occupying Belgium. The war, said to be 'la guerre aux rois et la paix aux peuples', proved to be Louis's death-warrant.

A Prussian force, under the Duke of Brunswick, moved into Lorraine and captured the fortresses of Longwy and Verdun and, in July, the Austrians entered France from the Netherlands and besieged Lille. But in September the Prussians were repulsed at Valmy in the Argonne by untrained and undisciplined revolutionary levies

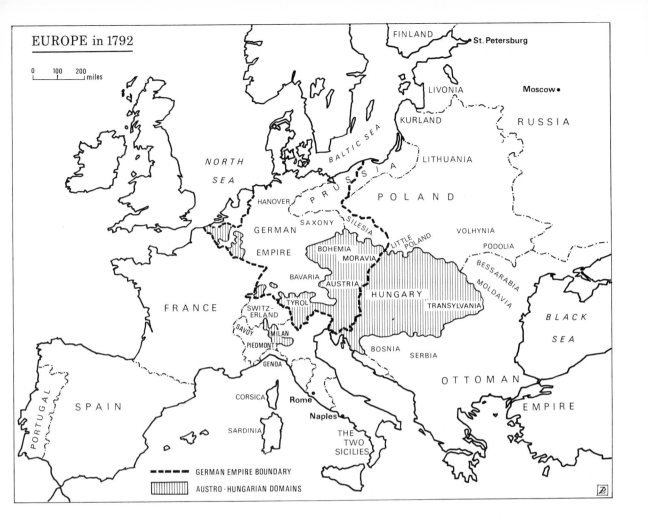

EUROPE in 1792

0 100 200 miles

- - - - GERMAN EMPIRE BOUNDARY

||||||| AUSTRO-HUNGARIAN DOMAINS

which had, however, the support of the royalist artillery; the Prussians withdrew into Germany, and the French followed up, occupying Mainz, Worms, and Frankfurt. The French commander, Dumouriez, relieved Lille and, invading the Netherlands, defeated the Austrians at Jemappes. Brussels fell and the whole province was overrun. Another French army, attacking Piedmont and the kingdom of Sardinia took Savoy and Nice.

Although news of the French Revolution had at first been welcomed in Britain, the massacres, the deposition of Louis XVI, the Edict of Fraternity aimed at inciting rebellion abroad, and the opening by the French of the Scheldt estuary to the shipping of all nations soon revived old fears. The Dutch were believed to be threatened. In February 1793 the French declared war on Britain and Holland and shortly afterwards Spain was added to the anti-revolutionary

belligerents. In the First Coalition formed that August there were no fewer than fifteen member states. These, however, were disunited and split by jealousies and there was bad feeling between Austria and Prussia over the second partition of Poland.

Both Prussia and Austria had underestimated the effect of the French national revival on the morale of the revolutionary forces and both were distracted by a common fear of the Russians to the rear. Austria was involved with the Turks. But in 1793 the Austrians in the Netherlands attacked Dumouriez, who had meanwhile advanced into Holland, defeating him at Neerwinden. Dumouriez then deserted the revolutionary cause and went over to the enemy. A British force under the Duke of York, joining up with the Austrians in the Low Countries, invaded France and invested Dunkirk. The Spanish

9

An officer, non-commissioned officer and a soldier (in fatigue dress) of German infantry

Russia. Prussia, more interested in spoils to the east than in fighting what it regarded as Austria's and Britain's war in western Europe, made peace with France by the Treaty of Basle, agreeing, at virtually no cost to itself, that France should remain in occupation of the west bank of the Rhine; the loss of the small Prussian territories on the river was to be compensated by the gift of other lands, the property of German princes. Of the First Coalition, only Britain, Austria, and Piedmont remained in the war.

The Rise of Napoleon

entered south-west France and British sailors occupied Toulon.

Defeat, however, only made the revolutionaries redouble their efforts and brought the fanatical extremists to the fore. General conscription for military service was introduced for the first time and nearly half a million men were called to the colours. This was a departure from the methods by which professional armies had been raised up to this time and was to revolutionize warfare for the next century and a half.

In a series of offensives from the autumn of 1793 onwards the revolutionaries drove the Spanish and British out of France and overran the Austrian Netherlands once more. The Duke of York was defeated at Hondschoote and the Austrians at Wattignies and Fleurus. Moving into Holland, the French then captured the Dutch fleet which was imprisoned in the ice. Holland capitulated and was virtually incorporated into France as the Batavian Republic.

In 1795, by the third partition between Russia, Prussia, and Austria, Poland had disappeared from the map of Europe. Austria already held Galicia (from 1772) and now shared with Prussia the ethnologically Polish territories. Kurland, Lithuania, Volhynia, and Podolia had gone to

In July 1794 Robespierre and the Jacobins had fallen to Barras and the Directory of five members. That October Barras called upon a young French general of artillery, Napoleon Bonaparte, who happened to be in the capital, to quell the Paris mob. Murat was sent at the gallop to Sablons for the artillery, and with his celebrated whiff of grape-shot, Napoleon blew the mob out of the revolution for ever. As a reward he henceforth enjoyed the support of Barras, was made general of the interior, and was given the Italian theatre of operations.

Britain, by virtue of its command of the seas, was unassailable, and by default France's main adversary became Austria. Austrian Belgium, rich in coal and localized industries, had already fallen to France. Milan was an Austrian duchy outside

Dragoons of the Anhalt-Zerbst and Royal Allemande Regiments, 1798

Kellermann and Napoleon in the south turned the Austrian flank. While the main Austrian forces were engaged by the French armies on the Rhine it was intended that Napoleon's Army of Italy, covered to the north by Kellermann's Army of the Alps, should enter Italy by the Mediterranean coast road. Since the main axis and lines of communication of Napoleon's army ran the gauntlet of bombardment and naval landings by the British fleet patrolling those shores, Napoleon made a diplomatic show of threatening Genoa and began overt preparations in Toulon to assemble a naval landing force, this to give the impression that he was going to attack that republic from the sea. Nelson was misled into lifting the blockade on the coast road and deploying the fleet off Genoa, while Beaulieu, the Austrian field commander, became convinced that the primary land threat would come from Genoa through central and north Italy, against the Austrian left.

The Genoa republic had made known to the Austrians Napoleon's demand that he be given the right to cross Genoese territory. Beaulieu decided to seize the initiative and move his main force of about 30,000 men through the Bochetta Pass towards Genoa. Meanwhile, 10,000 men under Argenteau were to advance from Dego and Sasello on to Savona in order to cut Napoleon's Army of Italy in two. The Austrians would then destroy the encircled right before driving the left back on Nice.

the Holy Roman Empire, and Tuscany and Naples both had Habsburg connections; the Papacy was unpopular in Paris and a French ambassador had been murdered in Rome. Italy was rich and ripe for revolution against the Austrians, the Papacy, and the Spanish Bourbons, and France had a liberating message to give the world. By this reasoning, not all of it illusory, the Italian campaign was decided upon.

In 1796 the Directory resolved to attack Austria both in Germany and in Italy.

THE CAMPAIGN IN ITALY

Genoa and Venice were virtually independent republics while Milan and Lombardy formed part of the Austrian Emperor's domains. Since 1792 the Duke of Savoy, losing both Savoy and Nice to the French, had been forced back to the east of the Alps; however, he had kept in being a large army of Piedmontese based on Turin. The Piedmontese army from Turin and the Austrian forces based on Milan had for two years repulsed French attempts to cross the Alps and the Apennines.

The French strategic plan, as agreed in Paris, envisaged Moreau moving from the Rhine and driving the Austrians back on Vienna, this probably representing the greater French effort, while

An officer and other rank of the transport (*Fuhrwesen*) corps, responsible not only for wagon movement, but for all artillery horse-teams

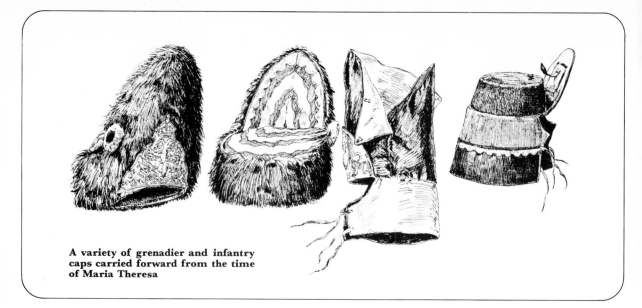

A variety of grenadier and infantry caps carried forward from the time of Maria Theresa

The two Austrian columns were, however, separated by a ridge of almost impassable mountains. Meanwhile, Colli's 20,000 Piedmontese to the west faced Kellermann's Army of the Alps. The French Army of Italy, although it totalled 60,000 men, was in very poor condition.

Beaulieu had dispersed his forces and was out of touch with the Piedmontese, and Napoleon seized the opportunity to defeat them in detail. Having left a covering force to delay Beaulieu's advance on Voltri, and a division at Ormea in case Colli should attempt to join up with the Austrians, Napoleon concentrated his troops under Masséna and Augereau against the Austrian Argenteau's comparatively weak force and routed it at Montenotte, driving it back to Dego. Thereupon Beaulieu gave up his advance and made off to join Argenteau. Napoleon then turned on Colli's Piedmontese and defeated them at Mondovi so decisively that Piedmont asked for peace.

The French began their advance towards Lombardy and the main Austrian force under Beaulieu. Napoleon had inserted a clause in his armistice terms with the Piedmontese concerning an intended French crossing of the River Po at Valentia, knowing that this information would be sent on to Beaulieu. The Austrians conformed to this false intelligence by setting up a defence line on the Po about Valentia, whereupon Napoleon crossed by stealth at Placentia, many miles away. Beaulieu was now threatened in the flank, and his lines of communication to Mantua and the approaches to Milan were exposed. The battle at Lodi, fought against an Austrian rearguard, decided Beaulieu to retreat once more.

Outmanœuvred, Beaulieu abandoned Milan and fell back on the fortress of Mantua and the River Mincio, intending to cover his own land communications to Austria which ran northwards

A field-marshal in the older-style Maria Theresa uniform, the rank being shown on the coat and waistcoat edges and on the pocket flaps. It was changed in 1798

12

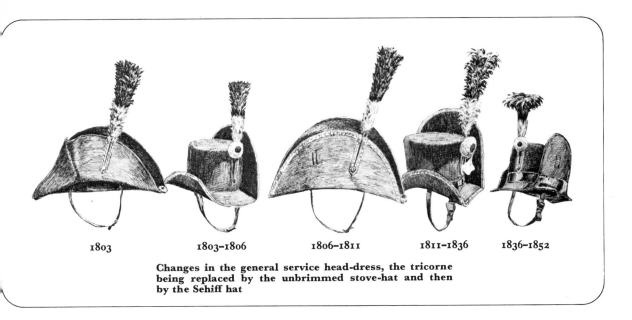

| 1803 | 1803-1806 | 1806-1811 | 1811-1836 | 1836-1852 |

Changes in the general service head-dress, the tricorne being replaced by the unbrimmed stove-hat and then by the Sehiff hat

on both sides of Lake Garda. He placed too much faith in the value of a water-obstacle and dispersed his troops into three bodies facing the main crossing-places. By a series of feints, the French had no difficulty in crossing the water and, except for the Austrian garrison left behind in Mantua, Beaulieu began to pull his troops back northwards out of Lombardy.

The Austrians, however, were not to be so easily beaten. In July 1796 a new Austrian commander, Wurmser, arrived in the theatre and began to move 60,000 men southwards on both sides of Lake Garda. The western column, under Quosdanovich, moved rapidly on the besieged Austrians at Brescia, while Wurmser approached from the east. Napoleon raised the Brescia siege and abandoned his heavy artillery; then, boldly making use of his tactical mobility, he attacked, firstly, Quosdanovich, repulsing him at Lonato and Salo, and then Wurmser at Castiglione. The decisiveness of Napoleon's successes had been unexpected in Paris and led to some modification of the earlier strategy. Napoleon was ordered to follow up the withdrawing enemy and enter Austria from the south, with the object of joining the French forces in Bavaria. Advancing rapidly up the Adige with only 25,000 men, Napoleon reached the Upper Brenta by way of Trent and began to destroy Wurmser's scattered Austrian forces which were being rested and reorganized. Wurmser, cut off from his base in the Tyrol, was

forced southwards where he found refuge by breaking into besieged Mantua.

Meanwhile, however, further to the north the French armies under Jourdan suffered two defeats by Archduke Charles, the commander of the Army of the Rhine, at Amberg and Würzburg. The other French army under Moreau fared no better for, having marched from the Rhine down the valley of the Danube, it was decisively defeated by Charles and was soon in full retreat westwards across south Germany. This put an end to the French plan to take Vienna from the west and south. Napoleon was forced to return to the siege of Mantua.

A new Austrian relief force totalling 50,000 men was raised under the command of Alvinzy, and in November 1796 this began its march towards Mantua in two columns, one from Friuli and the other from Trent. Napoleon concentrated against the eastern column and defeated it in a three-day battle at Arcola. Both Austrian columns then withdrew. In January 1797, Alvinzy returned to the offensive, moving his main force from the Tyrol between Lake Garda and the Adige, while a second column advanced further to the east. Once again the Austrians were defeated in detail as they came up on to the plateau of Rivoli. Some Austrian troops did in fact manage to reach the outskirts of Mantua, but both they and the garrison of the fortress were obliged to surrender.

Napoleon was now free to advance into Austria

A company officer and field officer of German infantry, 1798

October 1797 between Napoleon and the Austrians, the Habsburgs ceded to France the Belgian Netherlands and recognized the left bank of the Rhine as being France's eastern frontier. In addition, northern Italy went to France as a French-controlled Cisalpine Republic. The Republic of Venice, an independent state occupied by the French without just cause, was made over to Austria by Napoleon in recompense for her losses. Britain was the only enemy of France remaining in the war.

Napoleon's victories had been brought about by his superior generalship and, above all, by the mobility of his troops, a mobility which the Austrians, tied to the methods of the mid-century with a reliance on magazines and baggage-trains, could never hope to match. For Napoleon's troops ate by courtesy of the forager and the requisition form; for these supplies the Italians paid. At first they welcomed Napoleon as a liberator from the Austrian; only gradually did they become disillusioned by the constant plundering and heavy taxation.

THE SECOND COALITION

The Directory invited Napoleon to undertake the invasion of Britain but this project was eventually shelved in favour of an expedition to Egypt, which might, it was thought, threaten British India. Napoleon left Toulon in May 1798 with 40,000 troops and, having landed safely in Egypt, defeated the Turkish force there. A week later his fleet was destroyed at Aboukir Bay. Undeterred, Napoleon advanced northwards as far as Acre, on the Syrian border, which he failed to take; but there he found himself defeated by the waterless and inhospitable terrain, sickness, and heat. Finally he left his army to its fate (a surrender to the British and the Turks two years later), and slipped home to France. The destruction by Nelson of the French fleet at Aboukir Bay gave new heart to Europe and led to the formation of the Second Coalition between Britain, Turkey, Russia, and Austria. For the Austrian Emperor Francis II hoped to restore his fortunes in Italy.

at the head of a force of about 60,000 men. He was opposed by the Archduke Charles, the third son of Leopold II, a *Reichsgeneralfeldmarschall* of twenty-six years of age, yet probably the outstanding Austrian general of the time. Charles's force was inferior in numbers if not in quality. The French forced the Tagliamento and outmarched and out-manœuvred the Austrians. Charles fell back through the mountains and finally, when Napoleon was scarcely fifty miles from Vienna, the Austrians signed the armistice at Leoben. Bonaparte, who was neither a Frenchman nor a true Corsican, since he came of Tuscan stock, was master of Italy.

By the Treaty of Campo Formio, signed in

Napoleon, back in Paris, in October 1799 overthrew the Directory by conspiracy and armed force; a triumvirate of three consuls was set up, with himself as 'First Consul'. The so-called parliamentary republic had been replaced by a dictatorship. This was the first major step in establishing Napoleon as First Consul for life (1802), Napoleon, the Emperor of the French (1804), and Napoleon, Holy Roman Emperor (1806).

In 1799 the Austrians had an army of 80,000 under the Archduke Charles on the Lech in Bavaria, 26,000 in Vorarlberg under Hotze, and 46,000 in the Tyrol under Bellegarde; in addition the Austrian Army in Italy numbered 85,000. In all, they outnumbered the French who totalled about 200,000, not all of whom, however, were available for war against Austria. There had been agreement between Vienna and St Petersburg that the Russian Suvorov, called out of retirement, should be appointed as the *Supremo* in Italy, and that two Russian armies, with a total strength of 60,000 men, should be sent to Italy to assist the Austrians. All of these did not in fact materialize, but, without waiting for the Russian help, the Austrian High Command rushed into the war, expecting to have forced a decision before its allies should arrive.

At first Archduke Charles was successful. In 1799 he defeated Jourdan at Ostrach and again at Stockach, and, invading Switzerland, the keystone between the north and the south, he defeated Masséna at the first battle of Zürich. Once more the French under Jourdan and Scherer, unsuccessful on the Danube, were driven westwards over the Rhine. Kray, in command of the Austrian troops on the Mincio, was eventually joined by Suvorov, with only 18,000 Russians. The aged Suvorov was not without his former energy, however, for he defeated Macdonald at Trebbia, took Milan and Turin, and forced the French to evacuate Naples and Rome. But after winning the battle at Novi, the relationship between Suvorov and his monarch on the one side, and the Austrians and the British on the other, became strained; and the Coalition failed to follow up its victories.

Further to the north in Switzerland, Hotze and Bellegarde had lost their initial superiority over Masséna, and in the second battle of Zürich the Archduke Charles and Hotze were repulsed. In August Suvorov came north from Italy with 28,000 men and entered Switzerland, in order to join up with his compatriot Korsakov and a second Russian army of 30,000 men. But Korsakov had already been defeated by Masséna, the Italian Jew, who had served for fourteen years as an other rank in the Sardinian Army. Not a Russian gun or wagon had escaped. St Petersburg blamed the Austrians for this defeat, and the Tsar Paul withdrew from the war. The same day that Korsakov was defeated (25 September 1799), Soult, another former private of infantry, routed Hotze's Austrian force on the Linth.

MARENGO AND HOHENLINDEN

At the turn of the century Austria had 100,000 troops in north Italy and the same number in Germany. But Napoleon, who wanted to force the

Austrian generals in conference

main decision in Germany, had only 120,000 troops (Moreau's Army of the Rhine) immediately available. At the time it seemed that a French victory in Italy was out of Bonaparte's grasp since Masséna's force had been reduced to 40,000 men. With his customary energy Napoleon set about creating a new army, the Army of the Reserve, in the area of Dijon, suitably placed for use either in Germany or in Italy. This army remained under his personal command.

Some of Napoleon's generals were capable only of carrying out orders; others were exceptionally talented; none had the brilliance which he showed at this time. Although Moreau's numerical

15

superiority of 20,000 men over the Austrian force in Germany seemed little enough to ensure a successful offensive, for Napoleon, who 'relied on the mobility of his men's legs', this measure of superiority would have easily sufficed. He urged Moreau to concentrate his forces secretly in Switzerland and, crossing the Upper Rhine at Schaffhausen, to turn the Austrian left in great strength. Moreau, however, dribbled over the river piecemeal on a sixty-five-mile front, and started moving slowly down the valley of the Danube.

By then the Army of the Reserve had reached a strength of only 40,000 men and 40 guns, but Bonaparte began his march eastwards as if to reinforce Moreau. But, arriving in Switzerland, he turned south and entered north Italy through the St Bernard pass, and was ideally placed to threaten the Austrian rear. The Austrian forces were, as usual, much dispersed. Napoleon resorted to his customary strategic manœuvre and feint, detaching French formations to confuse Melas, the Austrian commander. This nearly cost the Corsican the battle which followed. For when Melas attacked on 14 June 1800 at Marengo, near Alessandria in Piedmont, Napoleon had under his hand only 19,000 men and 14 guns. Melas's force numbered 30,000 with 100 guns.

The battle began early in the morning and raged throughout most of the day. The French fought with great determination and obstinacy, but they had lost the initiative, and by the afternoon were giving ground. It seemed that one Austrian attack in strength would not only have decided the issue but would have ranked Melas in the annals of fame as one of the great captains. But the Austrian command was too deliberate, and its regrouping was dilatory. When at last the troops had been formed into mass column for what was to have been the final advance, a detached French division under Desaix arrived on the field. This was directed against the head of the Austrian force forming up for the attack. The Austrians were thrown into confusion; a cavalry charge of only 400 of Kellermann's cavalry caused a panic, which set off a withdrawal and then a rout.

By nightfall the battle was lost. In view of their numbers, the French casualties of more than 4,000 were severe, but the Austrian casualties were over double that number. The next day Melas signed the convention evacuating north Italy west of the River Mincio.

Meanwhile, Moreau, moving along the south bank of the Danube, had defeated Kray at Engen and at Messkirch, and in June he drove back the demoralized and weary Austrians from Ulm.

Bonaparte was without honour or principle and, bringing his own cunning and guile to French diplomacy, he quickly destroyed what was left of the Second Coalition. Promising each of the members the territories of the others, he sowed discord and heightened their mutual suspicion; and initially he was so successful that, in November 1800, Russia placed an embargo on British ships and trade, and Austria sought peace. Yet no peace conditions could be agreed between Paris and

A frock-coated officer, c. 1800

Horse artillery in action. These sketches are of interest in showing how gun crews were carried in the so-called 'sausage seat' in the gun trail

Vienna, for the Emperor was in fact unwilling to give up his English alliance and he had no wish to come to terms with Napoleon. But since the French were in Munich, Vienna was obliged at least to talk of peace. The negotiations dragged on at Lunéville until November, when Austria had concentrated a substantial body of troops and felt strong enough to take the field again.

Five French armies advanced eastwards on a line from the Danube to the Arno. The Austrians declared the former Parsdorf armistice, made in the previous July, to be ended, and assumed the offensive on the line of the River Inn. Two divisions of Moreau's left wing were surprised and dispersed into the thick forests, but once again the Austrians made little attempt to follow up their

initial advantage. Moreau withdrew and recovered quickly and began to concentrate his scattered forces in the area of Hohenlinden, bringing in 55,000 men of his total strength of 100,000. The Austrian field commander, the Archduke John, was badly served by his intelligence, and he believed that the French were still retreating. Of his total force of 130,000 men the Austrian commander had only 60,000 on the spot and ready for battle. John, in somewhat leisurely fashion, ordered the follow-up, but as the Austrian columns, winding their way through the forest, came up in succession, they were engaged frontally by the entrenched French. The closeness of the country made the Austrian deployment and control difficult. Fighting, however, was obstinate until

Moreau sent three French divisions to take the enemy in the flank, and these attacks, coinciding with a general assault from the front, decided the day. Moreau suffered only 1,800 casualties; the Archduke John lost 5,000, killed and wounded, 9,000 prisoners, and 80 guns.

Moreau advanced to within fifty miles of Vienna and the Emperor was forced to terms. By the Treaty of Lunéville signed in February 1801, France received the left bank of the Rhine, from Switzerland to Holland, while Austria retained its Venetian territory. Except for Portugal, Britain was without allies.

A month later the French Army in Egypt surrendered to the British and the Turks. Since Napoleon was anxious to repatriate the prisoners he determined to come to terms with London. This was done at the Peace of Amiens in 1802.

Bonaparte had no wish for a lasting peace and he regarded the Amiens agreement as a respite, the better to prepare for the continuation of the struggle against Britain. Among these preparations was the building of an invasion fleet in the French Channel ports. In 1803 hostilities were resumed, Spain entering the war the next year on the side of the French. The Battle of Trafalgar in 1805 removed from the British Isles the danger of invasion, but meanwhile London had entered into secret negotiations with Austria, Russia, Prussia, and Sweden, and British wealth,

and diplomacy were used to bolster the fortunes of these continental allies.

Austria was probably the most honest and staunch of Britain's allies. But the long series of defeats had made the Emperor reluctant to take up arms once more against the Corsican tyrant, however personally distasteful he might find him. And yet, once the decision had been made to join the Third Coalition, Austria impetuously rushed to arms again and took the field without waiting for the arrival of its allies.

ULM AND AUSTERLITZ

The Austrian High Command was mesmerized by Italy, and once more the bulk of the reinforcing formations were allocated to that theatre. Archduke Charles, the only Austrian general who had consistently beaten the French (but not Bonaparte), was the Commander-in-Chief there. The Archduke John had a further 25,000 men in the Tyrol. In consequence there were too few troops left for what was to be the main theatre of operations in Bavaria, where Mack commanded a force of about 80,000 men. Mack's army met an inglorious end, for in September of 1805, having begun to advance westwards across the River Inn towards Ulm, it drew upon itself several French armies which, by their rapidity of manœuvre, contrived to encircle an Austrian force of

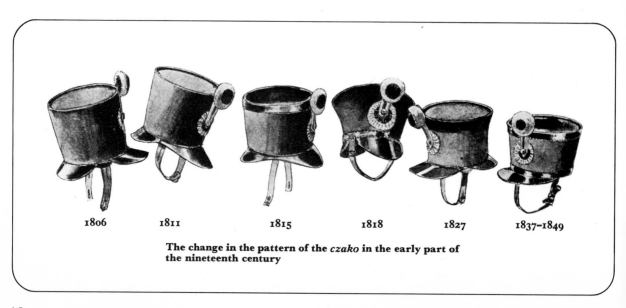

| 1806 | 1811 | 1815 | 1818 | 1827 | 1837–1849 |

The change in the pattern of the *czako* in the early part of the nineteenth century

**A cuirassier in undress and an officer in parade uniform,
c. 1800**

49,000. Only one division, under Schwarzenberg, escaped and made its way safely to Bohemia. The remainder, faced with great odds, were obliged, on 20 October, to lay down their arms.

Archduke Charles was ordered north with 80,000 men of the Army of Italy, but he arrived too late to save even Vienna from enemy occupation. He withdrew to Hungary.

Meanwhile, a Russian army under Kutuzov had been marching westwards in order to make a junction with the encircled Mack, and got as far as the River Inn. On the approach of the victorious French forces, Kutuzov retreated back into Bohemia and Moravia, where he was joined by the Austrian division which had escaped encirclement. A further Russian army and more Austrian formations joined at Olmutz, bringing Kutuzov's strength up to 90,000 men.

In answer to Napoleon's demand for immediate surrender, the Emperor Francis prevaricated. The young Tsar Alexander had been to Berlin trying to imbue a little spirit into Frederick William, the King of Prussia, and when the two emperors met at Olmutz Alexander brought the good news of a Prussian ultimatum to Napoleon, and the promise of Russian and Prussian military aid. Francis thereupon determined on striking a further blow against the French.

Both emperors thought they had cause for dissatisfaction in Kutuzov's conduct of operations. Kutuzov, who had served under Suvorov at Izmail fifteen years before, was a soldier of distinction and enjoyed much popularity among the Russian troops. This popularity was not, however, shared by the Austrians nor by the Tsar, who disliked him. Austrian generals, for the most part, were men of courage and honour; all favoured the offensive; their weakness lay in their indolence and in their inefficiency. Kutuzov was no Suvorov who moved only to the attack. Both Francis and Alexander insisted that Kutuzov should stop his withdrawal and bring his troops to battle. The Russian *Supremo* sulkily declined and had the conduct of operations taken from his hands by Alexander and the Austrians.

Bonaparte had arrived at Brünn in Moravia with an army of 100,000 men and, knowing that the Archduke Charles was near, he determined to bring the cautious Russians to battle. So he extended his 100,000 men over a frontage of ninety miles as if in an observation line, his dispersal being such as to invite attack. The Allied force clumsily ambled forward a little. Napoleon conformed by retiring, as if to encourage his enemy; at the same time he thinned

Light infantry officer and rank and file. Light infantry were the successor to the *Frei Korps*, but they were themselves disbanded in 1801

Infantryman of a border infantry regiment. These had a great reputation for marksmanship and fieldcraft

out the French right, leaving open the route to Vienna. Meanwhile, in anticipation of what he believed to be Kutuzov's attack, he rapidly concentrated over 70,000 Frenchmen behind the Goldbach stream. Then, as soon as the Russians had come down from the Pratzen plateau, he hurled his main force against the weakened Russo-Austrian centre.

The battle of Austerlitz began at nine on a wintry December morning and lasted only two hours. It was Napoleon's boast that out of thirty or more battles, Austerlitz was the easiest and most decisive of his career. Russian troops, temperamentally unsuited to fighting alongside allies, being by nature suspicious and obstinate to the point of arrogance, ran away, cursing the Austrians as they did so. Both Alexander and Francis had to flee for their lives. This was Alexander's lesson that war was not to be learned on the parade-ground and that he himself was without ability as a field commander. After the battle he wept, blaming Kutuzov for not having insisted more strongly on avoiding battle. For the

Allied loss of 26,000 men and 80 guns, the French suffered only 7,000 casualties.

Austerlitz did not, as Pitt forecasted, 'decide the fate of Europe for ten years', but it forced Austria out of the war and made the King of Prussia come to terms with Bonaparte with more than indecent haste.

THE END OF THE HOLY ROMAN EMPIRE

By the Treaty of Pressburg Austria lost Venice, the Tyrol and the Dalmatian coast (which had belonged to Hungary for centuries) and had to pay an indemnity of two million pounds. Napoleon, determined to destroy the Austrian hegemony among the German states, created the Confederation of the Rhine, a satellite *Bund* of German rulers dependent upon French protection, these having to find men, money, and supplies for the French Army.

In August 1806, a month after the Confederation had been inaugurated, Francis was induced formally to renounce his imperial title as Emperor Francis II of the German Empire, a dignity held by the House of Habsburg in an almost unbroken line for five centuries. He remained Emperor Francis I of Austria, a title he had assumed in 1804. The new Holy Roman Emperor was, of course, Napoleon.

Only Britain and Russia continued the war against the French, although in September 1806 the King of Prussia, goaded by the Tsar and smarting under the disputed possession of Hanover found an unusual reserve of courage and dispatched yet a second ultimatum to Paris, demanding the withdrawal of French troops from Germany. A reply was received within the month in the form of invading Napoleonic armies. The Prussians were defeated at Jena and at Auerstädt. At Auerstädt the Prussian forces had superior cavalry and artillery, and outnumbered the French by two to one. For the once magnificent army of Frederick the Great lacked any general of purpose and experience, and had been allowed to become obsolete and inefficient.

THE TACTICS OF WAR

In the early eighteenth century wars had been generally fought for limited objectives, and wars of position were more common than wars of movement. A complete defeat of the enemy was believed to be beyond the means of any state; the method was a war of attrition, and the aim the seizure of fortresses and key points to put one side or other in a stronger position to bargain at the peace conference.

The tactics of the day were dominated by the use of the smooth-bore musket, and the pike or bayonet; the musket, in spite of its short range, inaccuracy and slowness of fire, could be decisive if fired in concentration and in volley. The normal order of battle for musketeers was in line three or four ranks deep, and the deployment and movement involved had to be learned on the parade-ground by professional troops who devoted their lives to the service. Such professional soldiers were valuable and were not to be squandered, and Austrian generals in particular became a byword for prudence, believing that it was better to preserve their own troops than to destroy those of the enemy. The great Field-Marshal Daun was the protagonist of the creed that the defence was stronger than the offence; nor, even when pitted against a general of Frederick the Great's calibre, was he necessarily proved wrong. For he defeated Frederick on successive occasions, using the stonewall tactics of the period.

The French Army had declined since its golden age under Louis XIV, and it was left to Frederick the Great to change military thinking from the middle of the century onwards. For Frederick believed only in the attack, whatever the odds, and his audacity, coupled with mobility of movement, won him battle after battle. Yet in many respects even Frederick was one of the old school. He maintained the efficiency of his officer corps by personal example, by rigorous energy, and by meticulous inquiry, but even he took his officers from the nobility and not from the bourgeoisie: only rarely did he commission soldiers from the ranks. Close-order drill remained the safeguard of battle efficiency and, although he was not, on occasions, averse to eating bare the countryside of an enemy, he relied for supplies on an elaborate system of fortresses, state magazines, depots, and supply convoys, and was unwilling to venture his armies more than four days' march from a supply

A *Jäger* head-dress, arms and accoutrements, *c.* 1805

base or over twenty miles from a navigable river. His troops, like those of his enemies, remained long-service professional soldiers, although they were sometimes reinforced by mercenaries, by the enforced conscription of prisoners, and by national levies. It was Frederick's tactics and methods that were original, not his philosophy. And the Austrians learned much from him which they turned to good advantage during the Seven Years War.

From 1792 onwards the whole concept of warfare was radically changed by the French revolutionaries, for it was waged more ruthlessly and more efficiently as a conflict of ideologies.

The French royalist artillery and engineer corps had remained in being, together with most of its officer corps. The main body of the old infantry and cavalry had largely disappeared, however, and the new armies were formed by the *levée en masse*, a compulsory conscription of the nation's youth. Since there was no time to train the new recruits in the old methods of deployment into line of battle, the revolutionaries devised their own tactic of a column advance, with fixed bayonets, to

An artillery *kanonier* with a 6-pounder gun. An ammunition container is incorporated in the design of the carriage and trail and is covered by a seat on which rode the gun detachment

overwhelm the enemy line. A single battalion had a frontage of forty men and a depth of twenty-four ranks; more battalions could give additional frontage and depth. When ordered to attack, the battalion marched to the beat of the drum in serried ranks, rather like a phalanx or square, direct on to the enemy. There was no question of any use of musketry since the assault formation did not allow it; the men of the first two ranks might fire a round on closing with the enemy, but this was done on the move, and the rapid march-step allowed no time to reload. Such attacks, which were nothing more than marching right over the enemy, brought heavy losses to the French, but since men were plentiful and held cheap, this was considered to be of little account. Fear of the guillotine forced commanders to be energetic and casualties ensured rapid promotion.

It might be thought that the adoption of this new tactic was to invite disaster. Yet in fact the attack in column by untried and virtually untrained conscripts swept away the veterans of the Russian, Prussian, and Austrian armies. It appeared irresistible. There were many reasons for this. The closed ranks facilitated control, and no man could falter or run away; the advance of the column was covered by artillery at the flank and by skirmishers in front, who tried to break the enemy line by fire, before the arrival of the column; and lastly, the effect of the steady advance of massed column, together with the fire of artillery and skirmishers, was often sufficient to demoralize the enemy before the main battle was joined.

One by one, all the European powers, except the British, abandoned line and adopted the attack in column.

The French Army of the period was superior to

those of its enemies in many other respects. It had excellent organization, good armament, and had become renowned for its offensive spirit. Promotion was not to be gained by birth or interest but by merit. Its morale, after the suppression of the extremist revolutionaries, was excellent, and Napoleon was little plagued by desertions, the curse of the long-service armies of his enemies. Napoleon himself was enormously popular with his troops. Yet there was much about him of the charlatan. With his remark, 'What do the lives of half a million men matter to a man like me?' he certainly was not averse to the shedding of blood. Yet he lost more men in his rapid marches than he did in battle. For he was the strategist *par excellence*; the unfortunate Mack had been forced to surrender at Ulm in 1805 because no Austrian could conceive it possible that the Grand Army could march from Boulogne to the Danube, a distance of nearly 700 miles, in under eight weeks.

Since the French revolutionaries could not afford to provide magazines and baggage-trains they ordered the armies to live off the country, and

A cavalry charge by uhlans, *c*. 1812

to do this they had to keep moving, usually in the direction of the enemy. Napoleon continued the system, applying it more ruthlessly, and in the early years it was to enhance his mobility. Before the end, however, in Russia it was to destroy him.

When he was in his prime, Bonaparte probably was without equal as a soldier. Full of abounding energy and determination, he had profound confidence in his destiny and star, and in this lay the seeds of his subsequent defeat. He himself did, saw, and regulated everything, and generally robbed his subordinates of initiative. He failed to realize the deterioration in himself and his levies and the growing strength and the improving capabilities of his enemies. As time progressed he began to live in a dream world of his own making which had little relation to reality.

Bonaparte was a strategist rather than a tactician and much of his success was due to the boldness of his plans and the simplicity and speed with which he executed them. He relied much on the excellent marching powers of his troops and the surprise which these gave him, defeating his enemies before they could concentrate or join forces. As a tactician he was remarkable only for his development and skilful use of artillery. He retained his confidence in the attack in column (bequeathed to him by Carnot) until the hour of his final defeat at Waterloo, notwithstanding the defeats of his marshals in the Peninsula.

A cuirassier wearing the greatcoat which had replaced his earlier coat

Austrian Military Reforms

The Austrian High Command, in common with the other European powers, used the peace from 1806 to 1809 to good advantage. The Archduke Charles had fought his last battle in 1805 when, as commander of the Army of Italy, he defeated Masséna at Caldiero. Following the Peace of Lunéville Charles was recalled to Vienna and appointed President of the Council of War, and in this appointment he began his mammoth task of the reorganization of the Austrian military forces.

Charles had of course reached the rank of field-marshal at such an early age because of his royal birth. But he had acquired much experience, as a brigade commander at Jemappes and Neerwinden, and as the commander of the forces on the Rhine, and in Italy he had won many victories over Napoleon's generals. And he had the assistance in his new appointment of one of the most distinguished generals Hungary has ever produced, Radetzky von Radetz. A veteran of the wars against the Turks and in the Low Countries, Radetzky had served under Beaulieu and Wurmser and was extremely popular among the Austrian rank and file, an attribute, according to one Hungarian cynic, rare enough among the Austrian generals at the time. In 1808 Radetzky became Chief of the General Staff and Archduke Charles's chief executive.

One of the main weaknesses of the Austro-Hungarian Army lay in its multi-racial character. The steadiest and staunchest arm was its German infantry and this took the brunt of most of the fighting. The Bohemian and Moravian elements tended to be politically unreliable and more prone to desertion, particularly since the Austrian was often viewed as a foreign ruler and oppressor. The Hungarian was in yet a different category for he regarded himself as the equal if not the superior to the Austrian in war; in fact he was usually a better horseman than his Germanic neighbour but he lacked the self-discipline, stamina, and stolidity which make a good infantryman; and although he had bravery and dash, he disliked routine and application to monotonous tasks.

Yet although Hungary took its full share in the wars with the French, the national fervour and support which the Hungarians of all classes had shown in support of their Austrian Queen, Maria Theresa, were lacking. Nor could suitable military employment be found for the many minorities, particularly the Croats and the Rumanians, for unlike the pandours and irregular hussars of the Silesian Wars, there was no place for the many *Frei Korps* in the Napoleonic era. The *Frei Korps* were eventually converted into regular light infantry but, since they were temperamentally unsuited to this employment, they were disbanded in 1801.

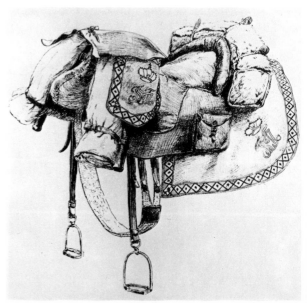

General-service saddle of the pattern used by most German cavalry and horse artillery

1 **Officer of Hungarian Grenadiers, summer field service uniform,** *c.* **1805**
2 **Private Soldier of Hungarian Infantry, summer field service uniform,** *c.* **1806**
3 **Grenadier of German Infantry, summer field service uniform,** *c.* **1809**

A

Mounted *Jäger* and Light Dragoon, summer field service uniform, *c.* 1800

R. OTTENFELD

1 *Jäger* Soldier, summer field service
  uniform, *c.* 1809
2 German *Jäger* Non-Commissioned Officer,
  summer field service uniform, *c.* 1805
3 Private Soldier of German Infantry,
  summer field service uniform, *c.* 1804

R. OTTENFELD

C

Trooper of Hussars, summer field service uniform, *c.* 1806

1 **Sapper Officer, summer field service dress,** *c.* 1800
2 **Miner Officer, summer field service uniform,** *c.* 1800
3 **Soldier of the Pioneer Corps, summer field service uniform,** *c.* 1800

R. OTTENFELD

E

Trooper of Uhlans, summer field service dress, *c.* 1815

F

1 **Soldier of Pioneers, summer field service uniform,** *c.* 1809
2 **Soldier of Miners, summer field service marching order,** *c.* 1809
3 **Field-Marshal, parade order,** *c.* 1800

R. OTTENFELD

G

1 Major-General, parade uniform, c. 1809
2 Corporal of Artillery winter field service order, c. 1809
3 Driver of the Transport Corps, summer field service uniform, c. 1809

The Archduke Charles's reforms covered both the infantry and the cavalry and in particular the application of their tactics. But it was in the reorganization of the artillery that he was most concerned. Charles had learned much from the French and he determined to concentrate the control of the artillery at the highest possible level. The line guns, previously decentralized to infantry, disappeared in accordance with the French practice (although Bonaparte was in fact to restore them in 1809), and the Austrian artillery was built up as an independent supporting arm.

In 1808 the Austrian artillery took into use the Congreve rocket, from which was developed a two-barrelled 5 cm. rocket. The launchers, which weighed only 19 lb. each, fired a 6- or a 12-pounder shell, twenty-four launchers comprising a battery. For siege work 16- and 28-pounders were also used. Rockets were originally manned by the *Feuerwerkscorps*.

The 1805 Treaty of Pressburg which had lost Hungary Dalmatia and cost Austria the Tyrol (ceded to Bavaria) was not to be forgotten and it left behind a passion for revenge. Although the Archduke Charles was to lose the next battle against Napoleon his work in reorganizing the army, and in particular the artillery, was to have a marked effect on Austrian fortunes in the next five years. For Austria had not ceased to rearm since Austerlitz.

The New Austrian War

In 1807 Napoleon had come to an agreement with the Tsar Alexander, but the peace they kept was an uneasy one. The French attempt to ruin Britain economically by cutting it off from its continental markets (promulgated in the 1806 and 1807 Berlin and Milan decrees) was proving a failure. The British had returned to Portugal, and Napoleon himself had had to go to the Iberian Peninsula.

When Bonaparte had met the Tsar in Erfurt in 1808 he had tried to win from him an undertaking that Russian armies would neutralize Austria, should the Austrian Emperor decide to go to war; Alexander refused to give this assurance. Napoleon and the French were unpopular throughout Germany and Austria where their talk of liberty and equality was seen to apply only to French citizens. In April 1809 the Austrian Emperor, Francis, with a recently found confidence in the new efficiency of his armies, and without seeking allies, as the German champion declared war on France.

The declaration was not unexpected, for Austria's feverish rearmament could have had no

A hussar officer's equipment and shako, *sabretache* **and** *cartouchiere*

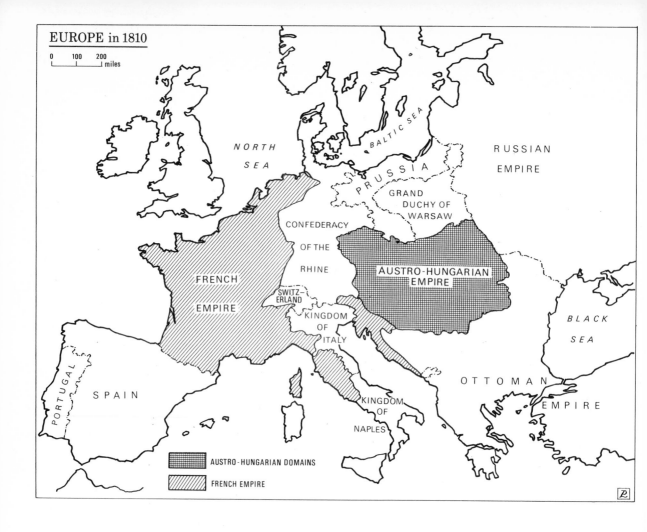

EUROPE in 1810

0   100   200
|____|____|____| miles

NORTH SEA

BALTIC SEA

RUSSIAN EMPIRE

PRUSSIA

GRAND DUCHY OF WARSAW

CONFEDERACY OF THE RHINE

AUSTRO-HUNGARIAN EMPIRE

FRENCH EMPIRE

SWITZ-ERLAND

KINGDOM OF ITALY

BLACK SEA

PORTUGAL

SPAIN

KINGDOM OF NAPLES

OTTOMAN EMPIRE

▦ AUSTRO-HUNGARIAN DOMAINS

▨ FRENCH EMPIRE

other aim. Napoleon advanced from the Rhine at the head of a large army and by his rapidity of movement outmanœuvred Archduke Charles. Vienna was abandoned. Two engagements at Aspern and Essling came as an unpleasant surprise to the French, and Napoleon fell back to the island of Lobau.

Charles had at his disposal about 200,000 men, of which 36,000 were horse and 23,000 light infantry *Jäger*, and 760 guns. His newly reformed forces were organized on the French model and ate on the French requisition system. A further 200,000 *Landwehr* were in reserve, although these were indifferently trained and equipped and had only a reinforcement value. As against this, however, Charles had been obliged to detach 47,000 to the Archduke John in north Italy and leave a further 35,000 behind under the Archduke Ferdinand in Galicia to protect the rear from

possible intervention from Poniatowski's troops in the Grand Duchy of Poland.

Meanwhile, Bonaparte remained inactive on the Danube to await the arrival of the reinforcements from Italy which raised his strength to 180,000 men. Then, emerging from Lobau, he fell on Archduke Charles's Austrian force which he outnumbered by nearly three to two. On 5 July the French won the battle of Wagram, about ten miles north of Vienna. But it was a hard-won decision and the Austrians had proved a formidable foe; and though they lost 36,000 men, Archduke Charles marched off the field with over 80,000 men in good order. There was no pursuit and no rout.

Austria made peace in October; it had to pay a large indemnity and reduce its army to 150,000 men, losing yet further territory – Salzburg, Illyria and West Galicia (Little Poland). The new

26

peace enabled Bonaparte to transfer 140,000 troops to Spain bringing the total there under Masséna to over 300,000 men. The Spanish War was already becoming what Napoleon afterwards called 'France's ulcer'. After Wagram the French Emperor tried to consolidate his own position and that of his Empire by divorcing Josephine and taking a new wife, Marie-Louise, Archduchess of Austria and daughter of Francis I. When his son was born in 1811 Napoleon re-created for him the old Germanic title of the King of Rome, used by the early emperors.

Francis had been valiantly supported by his Hungarian subjects, and 1809 marked the end of the old *insurrectio* militia when it came to battle for the last time at Gyor. Francis's courageous attempt to free Austria and Germany had failed because of the disunity and selfishness of the German princes and the timidity of the Prussian king.

Although Prussia took no part in the Franco-Austrian War of 1809, its army having been reduced at Napoleon's order to a ceiling of 42,000 men, the Austrian rearmament, and its effect, had not gone unnoticed in Berlin. Civil and military reforms were set in motion there by Stein and Hardenberg and by Scharnhorst and Gneisenau. Serfdom was abolished and the rigid class barriers removed; army officers were no longer appointed solely from the nobility and promotion was to be on merit, tempered by seniority. Arms, tactics, and methods were revised. But, most important of all, Scharnhorst hit on the obvious but no less ingenious scheme of the short-service engagement, which enabled Prussia to raise an additional and substantial reserve force, without exceeding the limits placed on the active part of the army. By this means Prussia was able to put into the field a force of nearly a quarter of a million men in 1814.

AUSTRIA AND THE TSAR

The Treaty of Tilsit made between Bonaparte and the Russian Emperor in 1807 had far reaching provisions. A new state, the Polish Grand Duchy of Warsaw, had been resurrected with the King of Saxony at its head, and this had been formed principally from the ethnologically Polish territories removed from Prussia. The Polish province of Bialystok went to Russia. In 1809 Russia, encouraged by Napoleon to do so, occupied and annexed Swedish Finland. Yet at the time of Wagram Alexander declined to give Napoleon any military aid against Austria.

Before Napoleon had asked Austria for a Habsburg bride he had requested Alexander for a Romanov. This had been refused. But no sooner had Bonaparte married Marie-Louise than the mistrustful Alexander became suspicious of Franco-Austrian accord. And, because he feared dissension among his Polish subjects, he had become

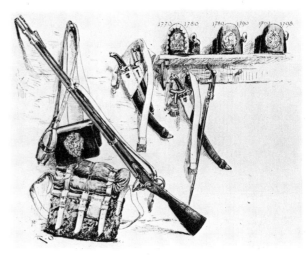

Infantry arms and accoutrements used during the French wars

very sensitive to the new Polish Duchy set up by Napoleon on the Russian frontier. Economically Russia was the loser by the new anti-British alliance and the continental blockade, since the main market for Russian goods was in Britain; the loss of customs revenues to the government contributed to the steady depreciation of the currency. At the end of 1810 St Petersburg, in a fit of pique against the French, replied by the imposition of a heavy tax on the importation by land of luxury goods, which in fact were mainly of French origin. Paris protested. In December of that year and January of 1811, Napoleon annexed to France the whole of the north German coast, including the Duchy of Oldenburg, which belonged by marriage to Alexander's sister Catherine.

During 1811 the uneasy truce with Napoleon became more strained and Alexander looked about for allies. The Austrian royal house, linked by

Miners and sappers at work wearing protective helmets and cuirass, *c.* 1812

marriage with France, was for the moment disinterested. Prussia was too fearful. Russia did, however, improve its relations with Sweden. Meanwhile, Kutuzov, in command in the south, was ordered to come to terms with the Turks. By the Treaty of Bucharest, Alexander abandoned the Serbs to their fate and gave up his conquests of Wallachia and Moldavia, keeping only Bessarabia, the eastern portion of Moldavia between the Dniester and the Pruth. Alexander then looked to Britain for another alliance.

Alexander had made use of the remaining two years of peace to improve the efficiency of his armed forces. In 1810 his main military adviser Arakcheev left the War Ministry to undertake the reorganization of the artillery and the supply of all warlike equipment. His successor as War Minister was a Livonian, Barclay de Tolly.

THE WAR OF 1812

The last approach to reason was made by the Tsar to the French Ambassador, General Lauriston in April of that year. Alexander said that he was prepared to accept the indemnity offered by France to the Duke of Oldenburg and would modify the Russian customs system which discriminated against French imports. On the other hand, he insisted on freedom to trade with neutrals as he thought fit and, fearful for his own security, demanded that French troops should evacuate Swedish Pomerania and Prussia. He went so far as to say that if there was any reinforcement of the French garrisons on the Vistula he would consider this an act of war.

Napoleon made no reply to these demands but kept up diplomatic activity merely to gain time, for he had already decided to invade Russia. In May the French Emperor arrived in Dresden preparatory to taking over the field command. Alexander was already at Vilna with his armies.

Against the Russian covering forces of about 225,000, Napoleon's Grand Army numbered over 500,000, but of this total only a half were Frenchmen. The remainder of his force were Germans,

Poles, Italians, Spaniards, Portuguese, and Croats, many of them doubtful and unwilling allies.

The Austrian contingent with the Grand Army totalled only 30,000 troops and these were handed over grudgingly. When Bonaparte asked that the Archduke Charles should be made available to command them, the Prince bluntly refused to have anything to do with the business. The command then passed to Karl Philipp, Prinz zu Schwarzenberg, an officer of cavalry who had seen service against the Turks during the war of 1788 and 1789, becoming a major-general in 1796 and *Lieutnantfeldmarschall* in 1800; his last military duty had been the command of a cavalry corps at Wagram. Thereafter he had been employed on diplomatic missions and had been the Austrian Ambassador in Paris: it was presumably because of this that Napoleon had asked for him. According to Austrian sources, he was instructed by Metternich to endeavour to keep his force intact and to give the French the least possible assistance.

Since the Austrian element of the Grand Army was so small a detailed description of the 1812 campaign in Russia would be out of place here. Napoleon entered Russia in June, but Barclay de Tolly declined to come to grips with the invader and merely gave ground. Bonaparte's progress was dilatory because he waited in vain for Alexander to come to terms. De Tolly was replaced by the aged Kutuzov who finally gave battle at Borodino. Moscow was abandoned and fired. Bonaparte stayed too long there before deciding to retrace his steps, and when he began his return march the winter was already upon him. Kutuzov's army was still in being and the terrible Russian winter destroyed the Grand Army. Very few of that half million returned.

The Battle of the Nations

Kutuzov, true to his nature, was disinclined to pursue the French beyond the Russian borders. Alexander, however, insisted that Russian forces should enter Germany, for the Tsar had come to look upon himself as the saviour of Europe.

In December 1812 Yorck's Prussian troops, without authority from the King of Prussia, went over from Macdonald's French corps to the Russians. Prussia welcomed the entry of Russian troops as liberators from the French yoke. The timid monarch, Frederick William, was forced to follow and, in the following March, declared war on France. Kutuzov took command of a Russo-Prussian army, until his death in April, when he was succeeded by Wittgenstein. Only, western Germany and the Rhineland remained to Napoleon.

By April, however, Napoleon had taken to the field again and at the beginning of May von Lutzen, drove Russians and Prussians back beyond the Elbe. Three weeks later he defeated them again at Bautzen, but this time the Russians yielded the field in good order and were shortly ready for battle once more. Wittgenstein lost his command to Barclay de Tolly.

Austria meanwhile used its good offices to attempt to arrive at a peace settlement. Napoleon was willing to talk, since every day gained strengthened his position. By August it was apparent that Bonaparte was disinclined for peace, except on his terms, and war was resumed, Austria joining Russia and Prussia.

Napoleon won the two-day battle of Dresden, but a few days later Barclay won a victory at Kulm.

The Austrian Field-Marshal Schwarzenberg, in spite of, or perhaps because of, his diplomatic missions, had always been an enemy of Bonaparte and he had been one of the strongest advocates for war against France when he had returned from Russia. In 1813 he was appointed Commander-in-Chief of the Austrian Army of Bohemia.

The Allies, Austrians, Russians, Prussians, and Swedes, with a total force of about 320,000 men were moving into Saxony. Napoleon had only

A soldier of the engineer corps, *c.* **1812**

190,000, but he was operating on interior lines and he intended to defeat his enemies singly before they should unite. Bonaparte's first intention had been to advance on Blücher's Prussians and Bernadotte's Swedes who lay somewhere to the north of Leipzig, but he turned off south-eastwards in order first to meet Schwarzenberg's Austrians who were moving towards Leipzig from the east. Schwarzenberg was in fact lying between the Pleisse and Elster Rivers in a disadvantageous and exposed position, but Napoleon did not care to attack until Macdonald should arrive. Marmont, too, had been delayed.

Meanwhile, Blücher, who was over seventy years of age and who had commenced his military career as an officer of Swedish cavalry, had decided that he could wait no longer for the completion of the concentration of the Swedish Army. Bidding Bernadotte, who had formerly been one of Napoleon's generals, to follow him when he was ready, he and his Prussians set off alone for Leipzig. *En route* they came across Marmont's force, also on the move, and a fierce battle developed about Möckern between Frenchman and Prussian. Bertrand's forces had already become involved in another engagement near the bridge at Lindenau, and it soon became obvious that Marmont would not reach Napoleon on that day of 16 October 1813.

That morning Schwarzenberg had given battle to Napoleon, attacking the heights of Wachau. At two o'clock in the afternoon Napoleon ordered Murat's 10,000 cavalry to attack Schwarzenberg's centre: this it did successfully and captured twenty-six guns. On the French side the battle then hung fire since Napoleon had quitted the field to see what was happening at distant Möckern, and Schwarzenberg's counter-attack forced Murat back and regained much of the lost ground.

During the next day there was a lull in the fighting and this enabled further allied reinforcements to arrive and deploy, Austrians under Hieronymus von Colloredo, Swedes under the Frenchman, Bernadotte, and Russians under the Hanoverian, Bennigsen. These brought the Allied strength up to 300,000.

Napoleon should have attacked on 17 October or have withdrawn; for when the Allied offensive

A field officer of uhlans on parade, *c.* 1805

was resumed on 18 October he had little chance of holding his ground. After several hours' cannonade the massed columns of the Allies started their advance during the afternoon, and by late that night the French were in full retreat, throwing out a 30,000-strong rearguard. So ended the Leipzig 'Battle of the Nations'. The total Allied loss was 55,000; that of the French was unknown but was estimated between 40,000 and 60,000. They left 352 guns on the field.

This ended Napoleon's political and military career, except for the brief 100 days' adventure which ended at Waterloo. In this neither Austria nor Russia were directly concerned. At the beginning of 1814 France was invaded both from the Rhine and from Spain. In March the Allies entered Paris. In the last resort Napoleon's power had always rested on his army and he abdicated only when his marshals would no longer fight for him.

The Plates

A1 Officer of Hungarian Grenadiers, summer field service uniform, c. 1805

The uniform of the officer of grenadiers had much in common with that of the officer of the line except of course for the distinctive head-dress. The main difference between the uniform of the officer and the grenadier was that the latter wore neither gold sash nor *porte-épée*, had no gold border to the peak of his shako, had ankle-boots instead of knee-boots, and the piping on his trousers was gold and black instead of gold. He had light blue shoulder-straps (the officer having none) and his cuff device, as with infantry of the line, was in white wool instead of gold. And he wore the private's infantry-pattern short Hungarian sabre.

A2 Private Soldier of Hungarian Infantry, summer field service uniform, c. 1806

The pattern of the uniform worn by Hungarian and German infantry was similar in most respects except that German line soldiers wore white trousers and black buttoned-up cloth gaiters which came right up to the knee. Hungarian infantry almost invariably wore the pale blue trousers, close fitting at the knee and calf, usually with light blue facings on the frock-coated tunic. The general service shako was similar for officers and other ranks except that officers wore broad (and non-commissioned officers thin) gold stripes round the top brim of the cap. In addition, officers had a larger cockade and a thin gold

metal border round the peak. Officers could be further distinguished from their men by black leather Wellington boots, worn almost up to the knee, a thin gold braid stripe on the trousers, and a *porte-épée* concealed by a gold silk cummerbund sash. With the exception of the shako, the non-commissioned officers' uniform was the same as that of private soldiers except that the sabre continued to be worn, although it had been removed from most rank and file, the bayonet henceforth being carried in a sheath attached to the bandolier. The field-pack (*Tornister*) was by this time carried high on the shoulders supported by two shoulder-straps, a departure from the earlier equipment which carried it at the small of the back on a single strap over the right shoulder. The pack was surmounted by a cylindrical waterproof valise. A black leather ammunition pouch was worn on the right side.

A3 Grenadier of German Infantry, summer field service order, c. 1809

Grenadiers were introduced into the Austrian Army in 1664 and originally their principal task was to ignite and throw grenades by hand. By 1750, however, they had become an élite shock force of infantry, usually a grenadier company within the infantry regiment, held as a

Hussars in plain smock tunic and cap (introduced *c.* 1815) and in parade/field service uniform

special reserve under the regimental commander's hand. In 1769 all grenadier companies were removed from infantry of the line and reorganized as grenadier battalions, nineteen in all, and these served as the basis for the latter-day grenadier regiments and divisions. In addition, the grenadier retained his specialized grenade-throwing function. The distinctive feature of the grenadier was his tall cap, bordered with fur with a cockade to the right and a metal badge plate to the front, the lining at the back being of the same colour as the collar facings. The short infantry sabre was always carried by grenadiers additional to the bayonet even though, from 1798 onwards, it was in the process of being withdrawn from German infantry of the line. On the chest of the broad shoulder-belt was the capsule case for the slow-match for igniting grenades.

B Mounted Jäger and Light Dragoon, summer field service uniform, c. 1800

In 1798 all dragoon regiments and the *chevaux-légers* regiments (which were themselves the successors of the horse-grenadiers and carabineers of Maria Theresa's reign) were amalgamated to form light dragoons. They retained the dark green coat of the former horse-grenadier. The collar and cuff facing for 1 and 4 Regiments of Light Dragoons were scarlet (as shown in the plate), for 2 and 14 gold, 3 and 5 orange, 6 and 8 pink, 7 sulphur yellow, 9 and 15 black, 10 and 12 sky-blue, and 11 and 13 pompadour-red. Where two regiments wore the same coloured facings, one wore yellow and the other white buttons, by which it can be deduced that the soldier on the right of the plate came from 1st Light Dragoons. The soldier on the left came from the Jäger-Regiment zu Pferd Graf Bussy, a regiment which owed its origin in the cavalry of the former *Frei Korps*, for the regiments Bussy, Rohan, Carneville, and Bourbon were amalgamated in 1798 to form a single regiment of mounted *Jäger*, eight squadrons strong. This regiment took part in the Italian campaign of 1799 both as cavalry and mounted infantry. The uniform colouring was *lichthechtgrau* with grass-green facings and linings, yellow buttons, green helmet crest, and black leather accoutrements.

The horse-furnishings and shabracks for both the mounted *Jäger* and the light dragoons were identical. In 1801, however, the light dragoons were split once more to form dragoons and *chevaux-légers*.

C1 Jäger Soldier, summer field service uniform, c. 1809

The former *Kasket* had recently been replaced by the black *Corséhut* (shown in this plate) with the left brim turned up and the cockade to the front. The uniform colouring was *hechtgrau*

A carpenter of artillery, possibly from the *Handlanger-dienst*

A light dragoon, 1815

so-called light infantry. In 1801 they were all disbanded. The *Jäger* was the skirmisher and scout who formed part of advance and rearguards and manned the outpost line. He was in no way an irregular. The distinguishing feature of the *Jäger* was his green collar, cuffs, and linings. His uniform could be sky-blue or *hechtgrau*, and the trousers were sometimes light green. Shoulder-straps were black with black and green tassels hanging forward on the left shoulder. He was equipped with a rifle, a long sword-bayonet and a powder-horn. Otherwise the *Jäger* equipment is similar to that of infantry of the line.

with the usual green facings and linings. The *Jäger* officer's uniform was similar except that he was expected to wear the *Schiffhut*, but in fact he often appeared in the *Corséhut* with a plume (*Federbusch*), either erect or hanging, fixed on to a gold *Jagdhorn*, with a gold clasp (*Agraffe*) on the turned-up brim of the hat. The officers' coats were supposed to be *dunkelhechtgrau*, but many retained the sky-blue pattern, wearing gold epaulettes (which were forbidden to *Jäger* officers) with black tassels and a green fringe. Officers wore gold buttons, gold *Achselschnure*, a simple yellow metal guard to the sabre, with a green and gold sword-knot. When officers wore the light green trousers they usually sported a dark green double stripe. Officers' waistcoats were white, fastened with hooks, their black necker-chief stand-up collars being colloquially known as 'parricide' (*Vatermörder*). Officers' greatcoats were grey with black cuff facings and black collars.

C2 German Jäger Non-Commissioned Officer, summer field service uniform, c. 1805
The *Jäger* was entirely distinctive and separate from the German light infantry, which was born from an amalgamation in 1798 of the many *Frei Korps* units of foot into fifteen battalions of the

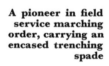

A pioneer in field service marching order, carrying an encased trenching spade

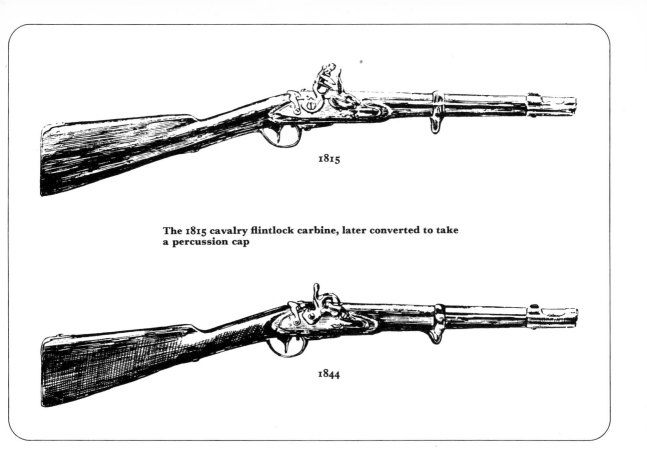

The 1815 cavalry flintlock carbine, later converted to take a percussion cap

1815

1844

C3 Private Soldier of German Infantry, summer field service uniform, c. 1804

This German infantryman wears the traditional white, with black gaiters and straw-coloured facings and linings. The pigtail (*Zopf*) disappeared in 1804 and the 1798 new-pattern head-dress (*Kasket*) remained in general service until 1808. The greatcoat was dark grey. The plate is particularly illustrative since it shows the detail of accoutrements, bayonet scabbard, water-bottle, haversack, pack, and cylindrical waterproof valise (badly slung and positioned). The black leather ammunition *cartouchière*, not visible in the plate, is worn on the right-hand side.

D Trooper of Hussars, summer field service uniform, c. 1806

The hussar, who originated in Hungary as a border fighter, continued to be the mainstay of the German and Hungarian light horse, for he could be used as line cavalry and yet apply himself to a dozen specialist tasks, in particular, scouting and reconnaissance, outposts and pic-

quets, escorting and convoying, and deep raiding. He never carried a lance but was armed with a carbine, a pair of pistols and a light-pattern sabre with the single *Bügel* guard. At the turn of the century there had been little change in the traditional dress of the hussar except that he had taken the buttoned-up overall trousers into use, these being worn over the boot. The shako, used by infantry and other arms, had also been adopted either additional to, or instead of, the fur cap and coloured bag. The circumference of the shako was greater at the top than at the lower hatband so that it presented a funnel-like effect; officers and non-commissioned officers wore the customary gold-edged peak and gold stripes round the top of the cylinder. All hussars continued to wear the dolman, *sabretache*, and leather ammunition pouch. The hussar horse-furniture comprised the regulation leather saddle set on a horse-blanket, with a pair of pistol holsters, cloak or greatcoat strapped across the pommel, and the water-bottle and spare blanket attached to the cantle. The whole was covered by the coloured shabrack and a lamb's-wool pelt, being secured by a leather surcingle strapped over pelt, shabrack, saddle, and girth. The carbine shoulder-strap fitted with a metal swivel, continued in use.

E1 Sapper Officer, summer field service dress, c. 1800
The duties of engineer (*Ingenieur*) and sapper officers overlapped, yet both were separate and distinct departments within the same corps,

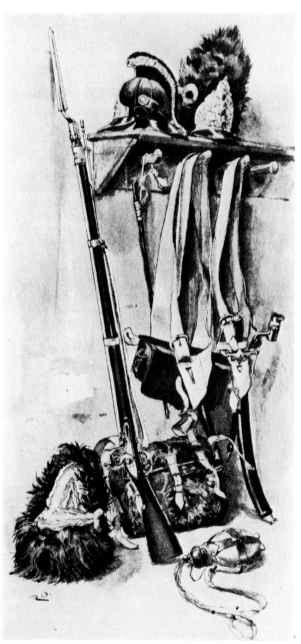

Infantry and grenadier arms and accoutrements at the turn of the century

officers and other ranks being maintained on their own lists and establishments. They took command over each other according to rank and seniority, but a sapper officer could not transfer to the engineers without taking a special examination or having served as an instructor in the Engineer Academy. Sapper and miner officers could, admittedly, be posted to fill engineer vacancies, but this could be done only as a temporary measure and when engineer officers were not available. Before 1800 it had been customary to recruit other ranks by transfer from the infantry, and in consequence the sappers received the unfit or the unwanted; but from 1801 onwards new regulations demanded that new recruits, direct from civilian life, should be young and strong bachelors, at least five feet four inches in height, and be able to read and write German fluently.

E2 Miner Officer, summer field service uniform, c. 1800
Engineer, sapper, and miner officers wore a very similar uniform, a cornflower blue or *dunkelhechtgrau* tunic with cherry-red facings and linings, and straw-coloured trousers and waistcoats, the buttons being of yellow smooth pattern. Greatcoats were of the same colour as the tunics. All other equipment was of infantry pattern. Miner and sapper officers wore the ten-inch high black and yellow plume, whereas engineer officers wore a black one (it can only be assumed that the miner officer in this plate is acting temporarily as an officer of engineers). The other ranks of both miners and sappers wore the *Corséhut*, similar to that of officers except that it was without the gold rank-band and had no leather edge, buttons, or chin-strap. The rank and file of both sappers and miners were dressed in *hechtgrau* throughout, with cherry-red facings (*Egalisierung*), artillery-pattern boots or twill gaiters, and carried a musket or a pistol in a black leather holster and an artillery sabre. The sapper sword was of a distinctive pattern in that it was saw-toothed for a length of fifteen inches on the back edge of the two-foot blade and had a modified haft and guard so that it could be used as a saw. The *Obermineur* and *Obersappeur* wore *porte-épée*, gloves, a hazelwood cane, and a woollen border to the hat. In 1801 the companies of miners consisted of four officers, two *Feldwebel*, two *Minenmeister*, two *Minenführer* (the

A transport corps driver leading artillery horses harnessed and saddled, c. 1815

sapper equivalent ranks were *Sappeurmeister* and *Sappeurführer*), and *Ober-*, *Alt-* and *Jungmineur*. In addition to their specialist duties they were used on a wide variety of labour duties.

E3 Soldier of the Pioneer Corps, summer field service uniform, c. 1800

The pioneers and the pontoniers had both been raised later than the other three engineer corps, and until 1809 the pioneers were under the direction of the general staff (*Generalquartiermeister*) and not the Director-General of Engineers, and because of this had green and not cherry-red facings. The pioneers performed many of the tasks done by sappers and their employment covered the construction of earthworks, fortifications, roads, storm assaults, demolition, bridging, obstacles, flotation, construction of accommodation and field-ovens, and so forth, and they owed it to Radetzky, who had once served in a pioneer troop, that they maintained an existence almost in opposition to the sappers. Another reason, too, which enabled the pioneers to remain in being, was that it was a Czecho-Slovak preserve, fifty per cent of

all recruits being Bohemian, thirty-five per cent Moravian, and only fifteen per cent German, its ranks being almost entirely tradesmen or specialists, carpenters, masons, millers, ditchers, and gravediggers. The pontoniers had a strength of six companies, but were not on the same technical plane as the pioneers on whom they relied for assistance in bridge-building; their only training was in elementary watermanship.

F Trooper of Uhlans, summer field service dress, c. 1815

The uhlan came to Europe by way of Turkey, for the word comes from the Turkish *oghlan*, meaning a child, and began its military use in exactly the same way as the Italian *infanterie*. From the border-fighting Turkish light cavalry, the use of the word and of the troops passed into the Polish Army, as the distinctive pattern of the head-dress shows, and from there, in the middle of the eighteenth century, it spread to Saxony and Austria. In the Silesian Wars the uhlan was often a mounted irregular as the hussar was before him. Eventually the uhlan became part of the regular forces (in the Russian, Prussian, Polish, and the Austrian service) and he

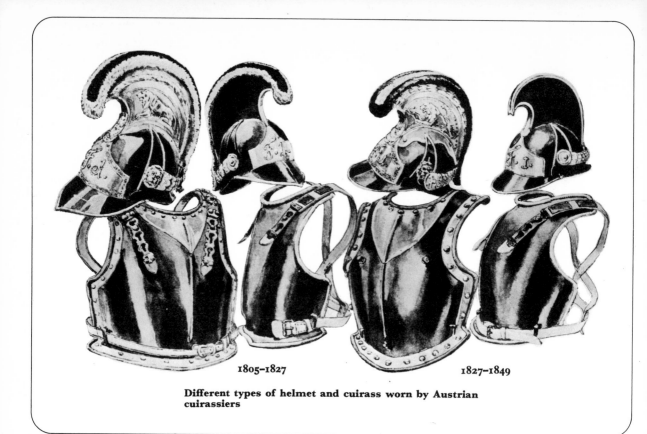

1805–1827   1827–1849

Different types of helmet and cuirass worn by Austrian cuirassiers

was in fact a light cavalry lancer. The soldier shown in this plate is possibly from the *Uhlan Regiment Prinz von Coburg*.

G1 Soldier of pioneers, summer field service uniform c. 1809

This plate is particularly interesting in that, in consequence of the 1809 reorganization, the soldier has lost his tunic and has been put into the general service frock-coat (*Rock*) worn by the other engineer troops; he still retained his green facings. He has, however, taken the new head-dress with the lengthened black and yellow *Federbusch*.

G2 Soldier of Miners, summer field service marching order, c. 1809

This miner is wearing the 1809-pattern uniform with the new infantry head-dress and longer plume, a uniform which, except for the distinctive badges worn on the side of the turned-up brim, was almost identical for miners, sappers, and pontoniers. Sappers, however, were usually armed with musket and bayonet and the short saw-toothed sword,

without the guard, pontoniers with musket and bayonet and the artillery short sabre, while the miner had pistol and sabre and a heavy entrenching spade in a leather case. Non-commissioned officers (*Feldwebel*, *Meister*, and *Führer*) were distinguished from miners by the carrying of *das spanische Rohr*.

G3 Field-Marshal, Parade Order, c. 1800

Until 1751 general officers had freedom to choose their own uniform and they wore what they pleased, and it was left to Maria Theresa to introduce a white half-length coat with rank designation shown by a broad golden ribbon stripe on the front facings and side-pocket flaps of the coat. This uniform remained virtually unaltered until the eighties, when the gold rank-bars were altered to a zigzag pattern and gold buttons, bearing an embossed star and an ornamented edge, introduced. In 1798 regulations for the first time made some distinction between field service (*campagne*) and parade (*gala*) uniforms. Greatcoats were henceforth to be *hechtgrau*, the same colour as

n by the 49th Regiment Vesque (later Hess),
.d-marshals wearing red- and gold-embroidered
.ollars and cuffs. The gold-bordered black general
officers' head-dress with the ten-inch-high green
plume was to be worn only for parades. General-
adjutants had the traditional green coat originally
worn firstly by the horse-grenadiers and then by
the Emperor Joseph's Chevaux-légers des Kaisers
(afterwards *Uhlan Regiment 16*). By an imperial
command of 1765 this coat was conferred on all
general-adjutants; it had the red linings and
facings of the original-pattern coat but with the
addition of general officer's buttons. The general-
adjutant wore a plain black head-dress with a
general's green plume; his waistcoat was straw-
coloured, with his rank shown by the broad gold

border stripes; the woollen breeches were of the
same colour. Infantry field officers' boots and a
gold-mounted sword completed his uniform.
Flügeladjutanten (A.D.C.s – usually to the monarch)
wore the same dress as *General-adjutanten* except
that they had white buttons instead of gold, and a
sabre instead of a sword.

H1 Major-General, parade uniform, c. 1809
The major-general wore the dress for German
general officers, his rank being shown by the zigzag
gold stripe on the cuff. Hungarian cavalry general
officers wore an entirely different dress, somewhat
similar to that of a hussar, with a half-worn *Pelz*, a
Kalpak with a plume of heron's feathers, a red
dolman, red trousers or overalls with a gold seam

A colonel of a Hungarian infantry regiment, 1798–1805

39

stripe, gold spurs, a red *sabretache* with the imperial arms in gold, and a sabre with a bright steel scabbard.

H2 Corporal of Artillery, winter field service order, c. 1809

As elsewhere there was a bitter controversy within the Austro-Hungarian Army at this time as to whether artillery should be fought centralized at the highest possible level under an artillery commander, or decentralized, all or in part, under the control of the infantry. The Archduke Charles believed that infantry should be self-sufficient and self-reliant and, when he became *Generalissimus* in 1809, the line guns disappeared and artillery became an independent supporting arm. Artillery was reorganized into field batteries (eight 3-pounders or 6-pounders), siege batteries (four 6- or 12-pounders or four 7- or 18-pounder howitzers) and horse-batteries (six 6-pounders). About four batteries usually made up a company and sixteen to eighteen *kanonier* companies made a regiment, although the total number of companies of all types could exceed this since it often included a *Feuerwerkscompagnie* for rockets, companies of bombardiers who manned the howitzers and mortars, and a *Handlanger* battalion. The *Handlanger* soldier was not a gunner or bombardier, since he merely acted as labour on the gun-sites and helped to protect the guns, yet in emergency he could often act as gun-crew. Austrian artillery was an élite corps and enjoyed many privileges, and from 1810 onwards, by an imperial benefice, it was given higher pay and pensions than the rest of the army. Artillery dress was the roe-deer-coloured

short tunic for summer wear and a half-le. mounted-pattern coat for winter, with the tr. tional artillery *ponceau-rot* facings (sky-blue for t *Handlanger*). The head-dress was worn with o. without the gold and black plume, rank being shown by the gold-bordered edge. A corporal commanded two field guns.

H3 Driver of the Transport Corps, summer field service uniform, c. 1809

The relationship of the Transport (*Fuhrwesen*) corps to the rest of the army was a little complicated in that, in addition to some general transport duties, it found the horse-teams and drivers for the movement of all artillery, to which corps it was closely allied. A *Fuhrwesencorps Artillerie-Bespannungsdivision*, commanded by a lieutenant with the aid of two *Wachtmeister*, had 70 men and 180 horses, but these were sufficient to move only three field (*ordinär*) batteries since a 6-pounder gun needed four, and a 12-pounder six, horses to move it. The *Fuhrwesendivision* allocated to horse artillery had 200 men and 200 horses, and this could move only two horse-batteries, three *Fuhrwesen* drivers riding the six-horse team needed for each gun. Although since 1772 transport drivers were permitted to wear the artillery *reh* brown, for the sake of economy they continued to wear the white tunic and breeches. Facings were yellow. Drivers and private soldiers wore grenadier sabres in a black leather scabbard, non-commissioned officers carried cavalry sabres and pistols. Officers wore dark grey uniforms with gold facings, and infantry-pattern head-dress, except that field officers wore no heavy gold edging to the cap.